FINDING THE ZONE

Sports and the Law of Attraction

GILBERT VILLALOBOS
ALBERTO FLORES

If you've wondered what it takes to be the best in sports, you have stumbled upon a great secret: Everything you have ever needed and will ever need is already inside of you.

This book is designed to help any athlete of any sport struggling from within. When you take control of your mental and emotional processes, you will learn to convert your fear into faith and your doubt into confidence — driving you to realize your greatest dreams.

The principles outlined will not only help athletes with their energy (how one thinks and feels), but will give parents a new blueprint to guide their children on their journey to becoming the best they can be.

Whether you play sports or not, our greatest mission is to enlighten your understanding of who you really are, and that you alone, control your destiny.

Introduction

Athletes around the world look for the secret to greatness. What do the greats have that others seem to be missing? What does it take to get over the hump and become the athlete your dreams are made of? What steps are necessary to achieve this legendary status? The answers are here in this book.

As you read, you will notice substantial repetition with our ideas and concepts, but this is for good reason. You will come to understand why later. From start to finish, this book will feed your conscious and subconscious mind to reprogram your mind toward success. You will also see major emphasis on how **thinking and feeling** and how it affects your performance.

For many people, competition is simply a physical thing. However, this book will teach you that the mind's role is as — if not more — important when it comes to your performance. Our purpose is to help you grow physically, mentally, and yes, even spiritually on your path to greatness.

Your dreams can be realized, and they will be — after you apply the methods and techniques offered in this work.

Our intention for writing this book grew out of experiences as both players and coaches.

Having played Division 1 baseball, collegiate football, and coached multiple sports for more than 15 years, we've learned how and why athletes fail and succeed in practically every sport and want to help you understand the same.

Many different topics will be discussed to guide you toward becoming the athlete of your dreams. Among them are the Law of Attraction, faith, persistence, patience, perseverance and a wide variety of other factors that either make or break athletes of all sports. Now, it's very important for you to understand the success of this journey has nothing to do with wishful thinking. Nor is it just about thinking positive and having everything turn out the way you would want to live. No, this is about fueling your energy to attract the life you want. Every single thing in the known universe is energy. Once you are able to change your energy, you are able to change your life. The invisible field of energy surrounding you draws in whatever it is in harmony with, good or bad. The forces of nature (the laws of the Universe) apply to all human beings. Whether you are a good person, bad person, or a combination, your life is governed by your mind. That is what you will come to understand as you continue on with this book.

I would like to congratulate you, as you have not stumbled upon this book by coincidence. Your search for answers has attracted to yourself the key to achieving greatness. Now, it is **your** job to apply the knowledge you receive, nobody else's. If you are ready, the application of the forthcoming information will enable you to become the athlete you have always aspired to be. Only if you are ready.

It is a fact that everything in your life, including what you experience in sports, begins from deep within your heart and deep within your mind. As you continue to read, you will develop the tools necessary to grow and progress closer to your dreams than ever before. I advise you to highlight as many ideas and concepts that speak to you. Look back on these phrases whenever you encounter adversity or when you feel discouraged. I am sure that when you do, you will find a spark again that drives you to keep pushing forward.

Lastly, before you begin the first chapter, grab a piece of paper and a pen. Not just a scratch sheet but something clean and neat that you can put in a safe place easily accessible to you everyday. I keep mine in my wallet. Now before you do anything else, I want you to write down your dream regarding sports as if it were already a reality. List as many details as you can about your dream. Where are you, what are you playing/competing in? What does it feel like? What does it look like? All of these details are very important. Your job is to read this paper aloud every morning and every night feeling every single emotion as if your goal or dream was a reality **now**, in this moment. When you've completed this book, there is no doubt you'll understand the "why" behind it.

Invest as much positive feeling as you can while you write. Know that when you have a strong desire, and you declare it to yourself and the world, forces outside of your control will begin to convert your dream into its physical equivalent. Once you have written out your dream with every detail imaginable, we can begin.

ONE

The Law of Attraction

"Your whole life is a manifestation of the thoughts that go on in your head."

— Lisa Nichols, best selling author, CEO, and motivational speaker.

WHAT IS THE LAW OF ATTRACTION? THE SIMPLEST WAY to explain it is to say that your thoughts and beliefs about yourself, the environment, people, friends, relationships, and the world, all attract to yourself circumstances and experiences which are on the same frequency as whatever you are focusing on. For example, if you think and feel bad, you will receive exactly that. If you think and feel good, you will experience the good which you have been holding in your mind. This may be a hard concept to grasp at first, but you will come to understand just how real this is, and how we each attract into our lives the things we think and feel about most.

Many studies have shown the power of this concept

including recent experimentation conducted by academic professor and engineer Dr. Bernd Helmut Kröplin of Germany which proved that our thoughts do impact reality. Kröplin's medium was water which, believe it or not, has the ability to store information given to it. Pretty cool, right?

Here's how it went. Using a dropper, Kröplin placed a single drop of water on a glass plate and allowed it to evaporate after it had been fed different forms of stimuli. Professor Kröplin had discovered with a dark field microscope that once the water had evaporated, the structure or pattern it left behind was in correlation to the thoughts, feelings, and information given to that single drop of water.

In this amazing discovery, you see how great the difference is between positive and negative energy. Drops that were exposed to "positive" stimuli had order and symmetry compared to drops that had been fed "negative" stimuli which looked as if a three-year-old tried drawing a snowflake. If thoughts and words can affect the structure of water why can't they do the same to us? Not just in a psychological sense, but on many deeper levels such as physical and spiritual as well. Keep in mind that scientists agree that humans are over 60-70% water. If this is the case, it would make sense that we either grow or disintegrate largely upon what we feed our own minds — or that which is accepted by us from others.

This is the Law of the Mind — the law that depicts your reality. Simply put, the Law of Attraction brings to you whatever you think about. If you think negative, negative things will happen. If you think positive, positive things will happen. Regardless of any circumstance, your thought depicts your reality. It's that simple. Why is this so? It is because everything begins in the mind. Every action you take, every decision you make, all takes place first in your mind. When we learn to use our minds constructively, we can begin to shape our own destiny.

Now, I will do my best to show you how this works. Despite the wealth of attention paid to the Law of Attraction over the last few decades, including the popular movie "The Secret" and many books on the subject, most if not all of them apply the Law of Attraction toward business and ways to increase profit. Since I have yet to see or read about how it works in sports, I made it my job to help you understand this powerful concept **so you can use it for the good that you desire** in any sport that you play. Whether it's football, baseball, basketball, tennis, hockey, run track, lift, or compete in field events, you will understand how and why people succeed — and just as importantly — how and why people fail in their chosen sport.

The mind. Within each person is a conscious mind (which governs our five senses) and within that mind is somewhat of a deeper mind which Sigmund Freud called the unconscious. Some call it the subconscious or hidden mind, while others call it the lesser or intuitive mind. Whatever you decide to call it is of little value. Perhaps the most important concept to understand with respect to the LoA and the subconscious mind is that although thoughts are hidden and silent, they hold infinite power potential fueling your body for action — which then determines your results.

If you hadn't already known, everything in the Universe is moving in a constant state of vibration. If you were to break down your body to the smallest particle, you would see that the atoms that compose your body are constantly in motion. It is the same with the chair you sit on, the table holding your dinner plate on which you eat, and the book you are currently reading. Of course you cannot see this motion with the naked eye, but all matter is vibrating at a certain frequency. Anything and everything you could possibly think of in the known Universe is in a constant state of vibration.

Music has its own frequency, just as water flowing in a river is vibrating at a frequency unique to its own nature. Even **your own thoughts** emit wavelengths which give off different frequencies. Once you have produced a thought, it is sent into the Universe, and that thought must return to the source (you) something of an equivalent nature. Therefore, thoughts and feelings of love produce circumstances which match that frequency. The same goes for thoughts and feelings of anger and frustration. **If you charge a thought with feeling**, the Universe, God, Nature, Law, Life, whatever you want to call it, will return to you the same which you energize. This is the reason you have, in your experience, everything you see before your eyes. Whatever you put out, you get back. But the emphasis here is working with your mind, where the work needs to take place.

Now let's begin to make the connection with sports. If what we think and feel has anything to do with how we shape our own lives, would it not make sense that our beliefs about ourselves also affect our reality when it comes to competition? Think about that for a moment. If I think of myself as invincible, as a force to be reckoned with, wouldn't it do me so much more good than if I thought of myself as weak or a complete failure? If what we think and feel shapes our lives, we could agree that thinking invincible would guarantee success over weak 10/10 times. Why is this so important? Because our most deeply rooted beliefs about self are controlled by the subconscious. They are the ideas that have been emotionalized with so much energy that they have made deep grooves in your mind that are almost impossible to remove unless you intentionally work to get them out. And the subconscious is the bridge to attaining everything you want. The Law of Attraction works so profoundly with your subconscious mind because it is how you truly feel about x, y, or z.

Here is an example. Have you ever tried to tell yourself something intellectually during a game or practice, but somewhere deep inside your heart you know that what you are saying isn't true? No matter how many times you tell yourself with your **conscious mind**, "I'm not going to mess this up," or, "I'm going to get this," you feel deep down that you are lying to yourself and that you could never do it. That **nagging voice** inside is your **subconscious mind** at work, telling you everything that is wrong with you, that you cant do it, and why you will continue to fail. If you do not know how to change this conditioning (which you have undergone for a lot longer than you think), you will stay stuck and continue to fail unless you get to the root of the problem. However, your subconscious can also propel you forward and enable you to succeed. Since most people don't know how the conscious and subconscious mind works, more often than not the voice they most likely hear and believe is the one that holds back the things they want to manifest in their lives.

I know firsthand how this works because the negative conditioning I received as a child held me back from pitching at the level I knew I was capable of when I was 16 years old.

After returning from a back injury as a high school sophomore, I tried convincing myself that I had no pain and that everything would be business as usual; I'd just strike everyone out like I always had. My attempt to convince my mind and my body that I was going to be okay only gave birth to guilt because I felt deep down that I was lying to myself. Since these firmly held thoughts caused guilt and doubt in my heart, I would go on to produce results which were in harmony with my feelings. As I said earlier, when negative emotions influence your subconscious, expect to reap negative results.

These habitual ways of thinking are otherwise known as paradigms — programs in the mind that depict exactly what will happen in your own reality. This programming, or conditioning, is the result of years and years of the same or similar information presented to your conscious mind, which, once accepted, becomes anchored in your subconscious. If you know nothing else about the difference between the conscious and subconscious mind, let me tell you now, that **your subconscious mind governs everything in your reality.** Since your beliefs are anchored in your subconscious, it can be difficult at times to change how you think and feel about a situation. I can now say from experience as both a player and a coach that this is one of the greatest downfalls of man. Not just in sports, but in every facet of life. It was just a couple of years ago that I realized this and how I could have changed my thoughts to eventually affect my own subconscious (which again, determines one's results). **This is key!**

Such may be the case for many athletes around the

world. The goal regarding the LoA is to bring to yourself circumstances, beliefs, and results, that are on the same frequency you desire. The bridge to your dreams is the subconscious mind, the starting and ending point for all things you wish to realize in your life. The Law of Attraction works for any or no religious affiliation, it does not care whether you are a good or bad person, for, "… He causes his sun to rise on the evil and the good, and sends rain on the righteous and the unrighteous" (*Matthew 5:45*). All that matters is **how** you use this invisible power. The power is in your own mind.

And here is where I want to leave this chapter. An important thing to remember about most paradigms is that they have been deeply rooted, even since birth. This is a clear indication of why so many children raised in negative environments go on to repeat the same in their own lives and in the lives of their children. Without even knowing, you have been fed information (true or not) which has shaped you into the person you are today. Having unconsciously picked up and emotionalized these suggestions — good or bad — they may have developed deep tracks in your mind which lead to frustration, fear, guilt, etc. On the other hand, you may have received information which has developed confidence, faith, trust, etc. Our job with this book is to help you recognize your deeply-rooted paradigms and accept only the thoughts and feelings you desire to carry on for the rest of your life.

Nobody wants to walk around with fear. You are meant to be confident, faithful, powerful, strong, disciplined, and happy. I tell you this because I have stated that your journey to success in sports is not only physical, it is, on a very large scale, mental. And yes, there is a spiritual side to it as well.

Not only do I want you to become the athlete you dream of being, I want you to become the best total person you can be as well. You have the ability to change the paradigms holding you down causing fear, doubt, anxiety and failure, into paradigms that produce faith, love, confidence, and success. Your spirit holds the keys to success because it is through the spirit (aka subconscious), that everything begins and ends. If you were fortunate, you were told by your teachers and/or parents at some point that you can do and be anything you want. There has never been a truer statement.

TWO

Faith - BS OR TRUTH?

FAITH PLAYS A CRUCIAL ROLE IN SPORTS. NOW YOU MIGHT
be thinking, how does my faith in an entity or religious
creed have anything to do with how I perform physically?
Remember, this book is not only about your physical
performance, but about your mental and spiritual practice.
What you think about, you bring about. However, I am in
no way interested in **what** or **who** you believe in, only that
you have **faith in something**. Remember that what we think
or believe is the most important thing. It is the starting and
ending point for all things including sports.

Faith, simply put, is belief in an idea. The thoughts you
hold in your mind are just thoughts until you choose to
believe in them. That's when they become a part of your
faith. You do not need to believe in a certain dogma or creed
in order to have faith. Faith just is, and it becomes a part of
who you are because **you** believe it. Why is it that the
atheist sprinter can be physically just as fast as the sprinter
who believes he has favor with God? The answer is not with
his/her dogma, it is with the thoughts and feelings that arise

in the athlete's mind. The atheist's **faith in his own ability** can be just as powerful as the **faith the believer has that he is favored by God**. This statement is not meant to degrade religion, but to help you understand that faith - whether it be in yourself, God, the Universe, a stone, or a brick - holds all the power you need to be successful; and just as important, holds the same potential power to cause you to fail. You can have faith in the good, just as you can have faith in the bad. You are free to believe what you want because you are a free being.

Here's a quick example. Say you have a big basketball game coming up tomorrow night. If your thoughts and conversations with yourself are **all** and **only** aligned with your desired outcome, you will be inevitably preparing your mind and body to perform in the manner you want. Why? Because, as Dr. Joe Dispenza, international lecturer, researcher, neuroscientist, and author of Becoming Supernatural says, "the body follows the mind." The reason for this, as previously explained, is because the Law of Attraction always returns to you whatever you put out. Faith in trusting one's own ability is positive energy, generating positive circumstances in return. The same works for doubt — which is still faith but on the opposite end of the spectrum because the athlete's belief changes from something good about him/herself to something bad. A thought has no power until it is believed. So keep this in mind: the next time you entertain something negative, remember it means nothing unless you emotionalize it. **You have the choice** to change your thoughts and believe only in what you want.

Recently I had the opportunity to umpire a club baseball game where Team Y was winning 8-0. Their shortstop was a phenomenal player and you could see that he knew it. However, when he was called up to pitch, he got into a bad rythm and started throwing ball after ball. No strikes. Bases loaded and the young pitcher kept walking runners in to score. The coaches and parents shouted nothing but negative things and you could see the pitcher's body language change from confident to miserable. Whatever confidence and faith this young athlete had in himself was shot and you could see a direct reflection of that in his performance. He was being heckled so much that he was literally on the brink of crying and this was one of the saddest things I had ever seen in sports. He was crushed. Instead of instilling faith into this young pitcher's mind, he was filled with thoughts of frustration and inadequacy. There must have come a point during the game when **he believed** these negative remarks. His faith, (which is only a thought, concept, or idea believed in) was no longer in the good about himself but in the bad. And as we have mentioned before, whether your thoughts are good or bad does not matter, the LoA always draws forth what you believe deep down in your heart.

You can guess what ended up happening with this young pitcher; the more negatively he thought and felt, the more negative circumstances came his way. His team ended up losing that game 8-10.

What makes this situation so unfortunate is that this 10-year-old, like millions of other young athletes, usually never forget the terrible remarks thrown at them despite their young age. Since willpower and focus are not as strong in early years, it is easy for the suggestions of others to become anchored into their young subconscious minds. These ideas, words, and suggestions become a part of their faith. This is why it is so important for you (if you are a parent, coach, or spectator) to only use words that encourage and uplift the children performing. The things you say can affect them for the rest of their lives. "You idiot!" "Are you stupid!? Get it right!" "You suck, I can't even look at you." Think about how a five-year-old will take that. You — their role model, father, mother, hero — speaking those words which can crush what you claim to love so dearly. You may think they are only words, but remember, once an idea has been emotionalized, it becomes a part of one's faith, one's life, if not able to be rejected.

Faith, as described in the example above, is one of the most important contributors to one's success or failure. The thoughts of the athlete who thinks deep down that he/she is too slow, too heavy, too dumb, too uncoordinated hold the same power as the athlete who believes just the opposite. The power, again, is in your own mind. It all starts from within. Do yourself a favor and start believing in yourself. This will be the first step to achieving greatness. It doesn't matter where you are. All that matters is that you know where you are going. Positive thoughts, mixed with faith will empower you to become the athlete you've always dreamed of. No matter what your circumstances, keep the faith in the good. Know, like you **know** that you know, that your performance can and will improve.

You may be saying to yourself, "Great, faith is essential to my success. But how can I develop faith in myself or my abilities? What do I need to do in order for my faith to grow?" As the great self-help author of Think and Grow Rich, Napoleon Hill said, "Faith is a state of mind which may be induced, or created, by affirmation or repeated instructions to the subconscious mind, through the principle of auto-suggestion." Faith, believe it or not, can be created and developed in your own mind. When information is constantly presented to your deeper mind WITH FEELING, your subconscious picks up these thought vibrations and proceeds to bring them about in your experience. With enough repetition, you will gradually come to believe that which you affirm and reaffirm to yourself. Once you have internalized the information, your body will follow your mind. So that statements such as, "If I touch the ball, I catch it" become true, and you are able to see it happen before your very eyes. That is what affirmations are used for; **suggesting to oneself** what one desires or wishes to be brought about. The more **feeling** mixed with the thought, the more it is believed. When you begin to use your affirmations constructively — as you'll learn in a later chapter — you will be using one of the most powerful tools in the Universe for success.

So take a step back and recall a time when you were preparing for a game, race, competition, etc. What were you thinking? What conversations were you having with yourself? This preparation (whether you believe it or not), had a lot to do with the way you performed once it was "go time." We will talk more on visualization in a later chapter, but I want to give you an idea of just how powerful faith is.

A prime example of faith in one's own ability is Muhammad Ali. In a pre-fight against George Foreman on September 17, 1974, Ali exclaimed, "I have wrestled with an alligator. I done tussled with a whale. I done handcuffed lightning, thrown thunder in jail. That's bad! Only last week I murdered a rock, injured a stone, hospitalized a brick! I'm so mean I make medicine sick!" Go back and read his words again. You will find that what he speaks only elevates himself. While some may call this arrogance, the fact remains that **he believes** what he is saying. I encourage you to stop reading and look up his speech on YouTube. You'll see a spark in his eyes that expresses only confidence and unwavering faith in what he is saying. He stated on numerous occasions that he was the greatest. Because he thought and believed this, **it became a part of his reality**. His affirmations became incantations (we'll explain what these are later), and his incantations, because he felt, knew, and believed them, became his faith. Something unique about faith is that it doesn't matter what someone says or thinks about you. What matters is what **you** feel inside. Here is where it gets tricky. Often people believe that just because they speak positively about themselves, everything will be butterflies and rainbows when it's time to perform. This is not the case. It doesn't matter what you say if you can't even bring yourself to believe it. Faith doesn't come from any one else, only yourself. So don't be fooled into thinking that if you can get **someone else** to believe what you say about who you are or what you're going to do, everything will turn out just like you want. **You need to feel it and believe it for yourself**.

If you ever have trouble developing faith, remember to be conscious of your conversations with yourself, and believe that you are enough — and even moreso — **you are already** everything that you dream of becoming. It's already within you. You just need to pull it out of yourself and believe it. Think and feel that what you want to happen is already yours. Remember that the subconscious mind cannot tell the difference between what is real and what is imagined. Your subconscious will respond to what you are feeling and thinking **now**. Not what you think about tomorrow or an hour from now. It starts right where you are and it is working whether or not you see, feel, or believe it. You will notice the thrill and beauty of this concept once you practice feeling as if the dream you are working toward has already been made manifest. Keep these thoughts, feelings, and beliefs in your mind, and they **will** materialize. The greats have practiced this technique for hundreds of years, and most aren't even aware that they've been doing it.

FAITH IS SIMPLY a belief in an idea, thought, concept, which has been fused with feeling and emotion.

THREE

Your Mind's Eye – The Key to Visualization

"Proper visualization by the exercise of concentration and willpower enables us to materialize thoughts, not only as dreams or visions in the mental realm but also as experiences in the material realm."

– Indian yogi and guru, Paramahansa Yogananda

EVERY HUMAN BEING VISUALIZES. IN ALL FACETS OF LIFE, we have taken the time to visualize something. Maybe it was job-related issues, a dream home, a wedding, a vacation, etc. What most people don't realize is that all of the images held in the mind make an impression on the subconscious because the subconscious' language is that of images and metaphors. This is how it interprets information. Haven't I mentioned to you just how powerful your subconscious mind is compared to your conscious, reasoning mind?

Here's a little something for perspective. In an article written by American biologist, Bruce Lipton PhD called

"THINK Beyond Your Genes", he explains that only 5% of our behavior consists of our conscious mind, while a shocking 95% of our behavior is derived from programming during the first seven years of life by observing family and the environment! More shocking, about 70% of this unconscious behavior is dysfunctional. This is why it is critical to feed your subconscious mind with only positive, desired ideas or outcomes. As you read in the last chapter, the more you emotionalize an idea, vision, or dream, the more anchored it becomes in your mind. When the desire or dream is strong enough, it will inevitably drive your body into action. Why? Because your body always follows your mind.

Likely you have heard about visualization before and maybe it brings up thoughts like, "Ah, that's a load of crap. I've done that many times before and nothing ever happens." There are a few reasons for this. One, be aware of the time delay that accompanies this great law we are speaking about. Many people give up on their dreams and visions because they don't think what they desire is coming to them on time. As philosopher and speaker Bob Proctor says, "Get locked into your idea and stay in that vibration regardless of what's going on around you." Find his seminars on YouTube. **If you allow present circumstances to rule your thoughts and feelings, you will never become that which you dream of**! Continue to hold in your mind the images you wish to materialize, and they will. **They must**. It is only a matter of time. Just be patient.

Remember that whatever it is you are visualizing in your chosen sport will not always happen to you or for you on **your** time. The Law of Attraction works on its own time, and the more you think or feel that what you are dreaming is too hard or too farfetched, the longer it will take to come into fruition. You cannot be hot and cold. If your mind has visions of desired results but your heart holds feelings of doubt, you will never bring forth the things you want. This is because your mind and body will be in opposition. Recall from the preceding chapter on faith that whatever thoughts, ideas, or concepts are believed in, will inevitably become a part of your reality. Believe that what you are visualizing has already happened. **Feel in your visualizations what you would feel if it were already brought about!** Your subconscious cannot tell the difference.

The other thing most people fail to recognize is that **we are always visualizing**. How many times have you found yourself "daydreaming" about something? How many times have you given in to these daydreams and felt fear when you've played events in your mind which led to embarrassment, frustration and failure? I can say with certainty that we've all done this at some point. For myself, there were times when I knew I was facing an opponent I had heard was bigger, faster, and stronger than anyone else we had played. The more I thought about it, the more nervous I became. And if you haven't made the connection yet for yourself, here you will see how your thoughts literally become things (in this case, a physical state). When entranced with what I feared, my palms might've started sweating or I might have started biting my nails. I may even have felt a knot in my stomach while in class. I pushed my body into a negative state by simply using my imagination. The things I worried about hadn't even happened, but they did in my mind. This not only caused my physiology to change, but it also began drawing forth more thoughts aligned with what I was feeling. Without knowing it, I was priming my body for the experience which hadn't even taken place yet. Guess what happened during game time. Playing quarterback, I was more worried about the oncoming pressure than reading the defense downfield. Had I caught and stopped myself from entertaining negative mental movies, who knows how much better I would've been once the game rolled around.

This goes to show that if you inject emotion into these sporadic fantasies — positive or negative — they will undoubtedly affect your performance in sports. The sooner you realize this, the more trouble you'll save yourself, and the more triumph you will experience. Go back and read this paragraph again. Then again. And again.

Earl Nightingale, American radio speaker and author describes this so vividly in <u>The Strangest Secret</u>.

THE HUMAN MIND is much like a farmer's land. The land gives the farmer a choice. He may plant in that land whatever he chooses. The land doesn't care what is planted. It's up to the farmer to make the decision. The mind, like the land, will return what you plant, but it doesn't care what you plant. If the farmer plants two seeds — one a seed of corn, the other nightshade, a deadly poison, waters and takes care of the land, what will happen?

Remember, the land doesn't care. It will return poison in just as wonderful abundance as it will corn. So up come the two plants — one corn, one poison as it's written in the Bible, "As ye sow, so shall ye reap."

The human mind is far more fertile, far more incredible and mysterious than the land, but it works the same way. It doesn't care what we plant ... success ... or failure. A concrete, worthwhile goal ...

or confusion, misunderstanding, fear, anxiety, and so on. But what we plant it must return to us.

SO THERE YOU GO. You have just become aware of how critical your mental movies are. It is important to note, however, that your visions without feeling have absolutely no power to manifest themselves. You must deliberately mix emotion with the images you are holding in your mind. Use this to your advantage. When you are visualizing a play, a pitch, a game, a race, or a competition, never allow your mental movies to influence your subconscious mind unless you want them to. When you are visualizing something you fear, immediately recognize it is only a thought and that it cannot manifest unless you continue to entertain this lie. **Your thoughts have no power unless mixed with feeling**! When visualizing desired circumstances, do all you can to add life to the thought. See the crowd, feel the sweat dripping from your forehead. See the lights, feel the grass or the floor underneath your feet. Feel what you would feel as if it is happening**now**. Experience the joy and excitement in your heart when you see in your mind's eye what you wish to happen. Your subconscious — your body — will bring it about.

By now, I am sure you have noticed the pattern of repetition with some of the words or concepts I have been using. This is no accident. You will come to learn that the more you read these pages, the more you will be influencing your mind in ways you never have before. You are now (without even knowing it) reprogramming your mind for success. This should bring you much relief, as **you have attracted to yourself answers necessary for your**

development as both an athlete and a human being. By the end of this book, you will have made new impressions on your mind. Your new and heightened awareness will allow you to view the world through a different lens and will help you visualize only desired outcomes. When you begin to "see" in your field of dreams visions which are not in harmony with what you desire, you will be able to recognize them and use what you've learned to turn them into something of your benefit. As you continue, if there is something that stands out to you, read it slowly, carefully, and with feeling. Let these words sink deeper into your subconscious so they make impressions on you which will last. Whenever you come across a moment when you visualize the **opposite** of what you want, you'll remember these words without any conscious effort. This is when you will know your mental powers have been strengthened. The mind, like a muscle, must be worked in order for it to grow. Make sure to practice the exercises we've given you and think deeply about the principles in this book. Victory will meet you with a smile.

If you doubt how powerful visualization is, go ahead and look up any of the elites in all sports. They all speak about visualizing — to some degree — what they now have. **They saw it before it happened**. Their dreams became a reality because **they saw in their minds what had not yet transpired, but had already taken place in their mind**. Your mind is like a garden, you will reap the fruits you sow.

Since there are so many different methods and variations to visualizing, my advice is to find the exercise that works best for you. Keep in mind that there is no wrong or right way to do this, all that matters is that you feel the reality of your desire as it has already happened, or as it's happening now — in the present moment. Visualization is the perfect tool for developing emotion because when you can imagine every detail as if it were right in front of you, as if the thing desired was already a reality, it would be nearly impossible not to feel happiness, excitement, joy, etc.

I have provided an exercise given to me by former NFL wide receiver, Super Bowl Champion, and very close friend, Phil Bates. My interview with him provided me with many of the ideas on visualization conceived for this chapter.

I was a quarterback in high school and junior college, always looking for the "right" way to visualize. What was I supposed to feel? What was I supposed to see? I had a lot of questions, and most of them were answered by one of my best friends who walked me through this exercise. Feel free to try it yourself. Make sure to read the example slowly and carefully as you "place yourself" on the field. You will be amazed by what you are able to see and feel. Notice your emotions as you practice this exercise. Know that you can use this for **any** sport. But let me remind you, there is no wrong or right way to do this. You can do it sitting, standing, driving, on the toilet, while you're jogging, etc. It doesn't matter. What does matter is getting your subconscious to see it all so that it will prime your body ahead of the experience.

Now, back to the exercise. These are the exact words my friend Phil used to guide me.

"CLOSE YOUR EYES. Focus. In your mind's eye, see the lights, see the field. Look down at the grass, smell it. Pick up your cleat and brush it against the ground. Feel the heat building up in your torso from your uniform and pads. A little sweat dripping from your face, no big deal. As you jog, feel the chill from the wind dry your sweat. Hear the crowd. Listen to the band playing while you're in the huddle. 'Okay... Trey left, 38 dice, on one, ready? Break!'

"'Go! 38, 15, cash! 38, 15 cash, set hut!' Three step drop, step up in the pocket, and completed pass to the post route, 50 yard completion. Now feel your heart racing as you jog back up to the line. Get the play from the sideline. It's high tempo. 'Go! 79, 88 money. 79, 88 money, set hut!' Drop back, side step, BAM! Sack! You know what that feels like. No sweat. His mama hits harder than that.

"Now back to the huddle. See coach's signal and get ready for the next play. A sense of urgency now, gotta beat the play clock. 'Alright, fellas... Trio left, 69 hash. On one, on one, ready? Break!"

"69, 88, omaha! 69, 88 omaha, set hut!" Read the two safeties rolling downfield, make the decision and throw... TOUCHDOWN! See yourself screaming as you run downfield! Teammates and coaches coming to celebrate with you. There's no better feeling."

WE CONCLUDED the exercise by having him explain to me that I need to see as much detail as possible. Everything needs to be crystal clear. If you have been wondering how people visualize, you have just experienced how easy it can be. If you catch yourself daydreaming undesired circumstances, immediately replace them with visions of what you want to happen. If you rehearse mentally — with emotion, you will receive whatever you have been holding in your mind and experience it in your physical world — but **you must put in the work**! The chapter on discipline will explain the importance of physical work, but what I am trying to get you to understand early on in the book is the power of your mind. Everything begins with an idea. This idea, if mixed with enough emotion, will inevitably materialize. Keep dreaming.

FOUR

Carry the Fire

The starting point of all achievement is desire. Keep this constantly in mind. Weak desires bring weak results, just as a small amount of fire makes a small amount of heat.

— Napoleon Hill

THE FIRST REQUISITE TO BE GREAT AT ANYTHING IS TO love it. Love is what will allow you to be the best you can possibly be at whatever you choose to do. Take a second to reflect and look back on something you have loved in your life. This can be tricky in today's society because the "L" word is tossed around so much. "I love this tv show" or "I love this color" or "I love these shoes" is not what we are looking for. We are looking for love in the most real, honest, pure, and sincere form. If you have ever loved anything so much in your life that it feels as if a fire is consuming your very being, you have found that thing which will allow you to push aside every obstacle in order to keep or obtain it. This is known as carrying the fire. This is true love. How often do you think about it? What would you do to get it? Before you proceed with this chapter, I would like for you to take a couple of minutes to dive into the following exercise.

First, I want you to think about "that thing" you really love. Think about every detail. This could be a person, a place, or a thing. If you are questioning whether you really love it, chances are you don't, so you need to dig even deeper into your heart to find it. It should come to you naturally because the first thing that pops into your head when you read this will most likely be it. It is important you find something you sincerely love for this first step because the next step will allow you to **feel** the emotions necessary for the success of the exercise.

Once you have found "it", imagine it in front of you, imagine you are occupied with or by it. Next, I want you to recall every single detail about this thing you so dearly love. See it vividly in your mind. What does it look like? What does it smell like? What sounds accompany it? Imagine everything to the tee. You should see it in your imagination as if it were right in front of you. Take a couple minutes here to really soak it all in.

If you have visualized fully, you will have inevitably triggered a variety of emotions. If not, try the exercise again. This time feel and see everything as if it were in front of you now. Think of all the things you love about this person, place or thing and don't forget to include every detail!

For the most part, I'm sure what you so dearly love will have brought you excitement, passion, desire, energy, amazement, hope, happiness, or any other **positive** emotion you could think of. It may have even given rise to emotions such as fear, anxiety, or nervousness. That's okay. You will come to learn how to change these negative feelings into positive ones, ensuring that you send out only desired vibrations which the LoA will return to you. Whatever the case may be, if you truly thought about something you love with every cell, muscle, and fiber of your being, if you have imagined something in your mind that your soul absolutely longs for, you have found a beautiful secret. **The intensity of your feelings for what you just imagined must be equivalent to the feelings you get when you perform or even think about your particular sport.** If you cannot make the connection here, you probably don't love the game as much as you say you do. And if that is the case, it might not feel all warm and fuzzy inside when you read this next sentence. **You will never realize your greatest potential at any competitive activity unless you truly love it**!

So many athletes fail to realize their greatest potential because they don't really love their sport as much as they say (or even think). This may be hard to swallow, but the truth is that the small percentage of athletes who do make it to the top will all tell you about the gruesome grind it took to get there. Their love for the game always exceeded any failure, setback, or task presented on their journey to success. When you are carrying the fire for what you love, any seemingly "negative" experience you come across will be miniscule compared to your dream. You will unconsciously be continuing forward because your body always follows your mind. If your mind is fixated on your dream, there is no possible way you could ever give up. Remember this the next time you come across what Napoleon Hill calls a "temporary defeat".

Dreams are not easily attained because of the hard work necessary. That was an understatement. **Dreams are not easily attained because of the constant struggles,**

setbacks, temporary failures, criticisms, and hard work required before the beauty of realizing one's dream. Keep in mind that whenever you fail, it is only temporary defeat. If your desire is to be great at your sport, you cannot let anything drive you away from your passion. So again, as long as you keep the desired outcome in mind — with persistence — **it will materialize**.

I want to leave you with a final point about your love for your sport. You can love something with all of your heart and experience the best that it has to offer, but you can also love something with all you've got and experience some of the worst this thing (sports in this case) has to offer. Reason being, your subconscious mind may know you love something (which is a positive vibration), but you can at the same time be attracting negative experiences in your chosen arena because of your fear of losing or failing. **You cannot fool your subconscious mind**! Starting from a state of lack, loss, fear, or limitation will not bring about the desired result. Learn to think and visualize only desired outcomes with what you play/compete in. Pour love and appreciation into what you do and you will see wonders happen. Love your sport. Know everything about it. Take care of it, and it will take care of you. The more love, passion, and desire invested in what you do, the more it will be returned to you.

One of the most beautiful things about sports that so many people fail to recognize is the beauty of losing. For most, losing has such a negative connotation that whenever it happens, they fail to see any good it brings about. Losing brings growth, learning-experiences, and improvement in many areas of one's life. Learn to love the game even when you lose. And don't get confused, the sport you play is only a mirror by which the game of life is played. When you are able to learn a valuable lesson about some aspect of yourself, you can and will always carry that lesson and use it in other areas of your life. What a blessing! The next time you miss that game-winning shot or give up that walk-off homerun, know that what you just experienced was a gift; something valuable that is only going to make you better. One of my coaches once told me, "You are who you are on the field". Meaning, that if you are tough as nails out on the field or court or gym or wherever it is you are competing, it is more likely than not that you will be the same way in other areas of your life. If you are hard-working, it usually translates into what you do outside of sports. The same goes for being lazy or indecisive.

Other than learning from your mistakes, losing allows for more fuel to be added to the fire! It motivates, inspires us to take action, it lights the flame deep within us to **want** to be bigger, faster, stronger. Sometimes, losing is the only thing that will give you the extra push you need to be legendary. Losing is only an avenue for change! When you can learn to look at a loss or temporary defeat as a gift, you will never again fall victim to letting negativity overtake you. This new perspective will allow you to be grateful for even the seemingly bad moments because **life is always working for you.**

Ask the elites of any sport, and many will tell you that some form of loss, humiliation, or failure drove them to elevate their abilities to heights they never knew they could reach. Michael Jordan was cut from his high school JV basketball team. Tom Brady was drafted 199 overall in the 6th round, James Abbott (Major League Baseball pitcher) was born with one hand. Most, if not all athletes have had to deal with adversity in some way, shape or form. Your passion and desire will enable you to keep pushing forward.

As this chapter explains the importance of what it means to truly love a sport, I would also like to send a message to both you (the athlete), and any parent figure reading this book. Sometimes, you just won't be able to bring yourself to love tennis. Maybe you won't ever bring yourself to love basketball. Your son or daughter may not love the sports you sign them up for. If the love is not there, you (or your child) will never give it 100% effort. That's okay, because the goal is to find what your passion and dedicate your life to it.

If you ever want to see what it truly means to carry the fire, watch Tom Brady, Serena Williams, Kobe Bryant, Alex Morgan, Muhammad Ali, Danica Patrick, Usain Bolt, or Lionel Messi. It's not hard to recognize the love when you see it.

FIVE

Stick-to-it-iveness

"A quitter never wins and a winner never quits."

— *Napoleon Hill*

PERSISTENCE, PLAINLY PUT, IS NEVER GIVING UP. YOU must keep going in order to reach your potential. No matter the circumstances, keep on keeping on. Remember that once you have created a picture in your mind, it is **your** job, and nobody else's, to make the dream a reality.

If you haven't already experienced it, you will surely meet adversity on your journey to success. Tennis, track, football, baseball, hockey and every other sport, just as every facet of life, will bring along some adversity. Every athlete you can think of or look up to could tell you of times in their career when they struggled immensely. More often than not, most elite athletes have all had moments when they thought about quitting. For whatever reason, one of our greatest gifts in life is adversity because it forces us to grow. As you will read in the chapter on patience, delays (or

temporary failures) during your journey will accelerate the fire within you. Adversity is a teacher and a good friend because if you were on a "high" all the time, you'd have no incentive to grow. It is a well known fact that a person learns more in their valleys than in their peaks. Keep going. If you persist, a way will be made.

"When you want something, all the universe conspires to help you achieve it"

— Paul Coelho, author of The Alchemist.

RECALL from the chapters on the LoA and faith that whatever you think and feel will return to you in equal amounts. When your journey tends to get a little bumpy, you need to remember that the most important thing is the end result you desire. Persistence, when it is fueled with faith, allows you to continue pushing forward. Your love and passion will not allow you to quit. The elites were able to push through, regardless of impending circumstances, because of the obsession they developed for their dreams.

Jesse Owens, the African-American track and field athlete in the 1930s is a perfect example of what it means to be persistent. His name would not be known had he surrendered into living the life of picking 100 pounds of cotton each day at age 7 — as had his former generations. You would not know "The Buckeye Bullet" (Owens nickname) had he allowed the negative treatment by white men to stop him from running. You would know nothing about the African-American man from Oakville, Alabama had he stopped running after a severe tailbone injury.

Thankfully, he healed and ran on to tie a world record in the 100 yard dash. The four-time Olympic gold medalist became a legend because he never quit — continuously pushing toward his dream. Remember, **your outside circumstances mean absolutely nothing when you persist in realizing the images held in your mind.** The Buckeye Bullet's legacy also includes some very important words which validate our core message in this book. Owen's said, "The battles that count aren't the ones for gold medals. The struggles within yourself—the invisible, inevitable battles inside all of us— that's where it's at."

So you see, it all starts from within. It all begins in your mind. The Universe will conform to what you want as long as you release energy that is in harmony with your intention. Do not be like the man who dug to find gold and stopped only three feet short of it. Be the person who continues to dig, even when the world seems to be screaming that you can't or shouldn't. The Universe will conform to the nature of your thought — **when you mix it with strong elevated emotions**.

So I tell you, wherever you are right now with your sport, whether you are currently in a "slump" or if you are on a high, whether you've been awarded an athletic scholarship or cut from the team, keep going. If your desire truly is as great as you claim it is (which may take some self-reflection), if your desire to realize your dream is true, then do yourself a favor and keep pushing. The Invisible Power that makes a way each time there seems to be none will open a door, paving the way to your reward.

I have experienced the power of persistence in my life as well. When I was younger, I was always told the odds were stacked against me. Supposedly too small, too weak, too blah blah blah. I needed only one person to believe in me, my brother. My brother taught me to shut out the naysayers and continue toward my dream of becoming a Division 1 baseball player. And it did happen for me, a Hispanic, 5'11" kid from a low-income family, a kid who was lucky to get just a single pair of shoes for the whole school year. It happened to me, after a major injury to my sciatic nerve kept me out for my entire freshmen college season. What helped me to stay on course? Transforming any negativity into something good. Even if it burned deep down inside, I would do everything in my power to convert that negativity into fuel. It happened to a pitcher who went from throwing 90mph to only about 75mph after my injuries began in high school. My dream was to become a Division 1 baseball player. As a community college student-athlete I had to prove I could compete at a high level. Having been recruited from University of California, Santa Barbara, University of Central Florida, and California State University, Northridge , I went to Los Angeles Valley College and continued **knowing**, **believing** what I dreamed about since I was seven years old was still going to happen.

I think the problem with many athletes is that they end up focusing only on the negative side of things. Have you ever been in a situation where you felt so uncomfortable that all you did was think about your discomfort, making it even worse? No matter what you try, the thought lingers and lingers until it consumes you and you become blind, unable to see the positive side it brings. Perhaps you can't even think straight. Life coach, Tony Robbins, says that even problems are gifts if you can perceive them as such. Remember always that the solution to whatever is troubling you lies within the problem. Can't lift the weight? Focus on your technique and form. Can't throw the strike? See the spot and locate your pitch. Missing all your shots? Focus on making them. Energy flows where attention goes. If your focus is stuck on all of the negatives your problem brings, you can only get results of the same kind: negative.

Train your mind to see the good in absolutely every situation. This won't be easy, as your mind may be clouded by thoughts of fear, anxiety, and frustration. But as you continue to practice, your eyes will see color. You will notice that every setback is actually an opportunity for a comeback. Every failure brings with it an equivalent success. Focus and be grateful for the good til your persistence grows stronger within you.

The reason it may be so hard for you at first to shift your attention from something negative to something positive, is because of the mental programming that took place from birth to about age seven. As previously stated, the repetition of information presented to you in earlier years may be why you cannot get yourself to see things differently. However, you can change this paradigm by using your thoughts to change the way you are currently feeling. When you are hit by some "thing" that makes you feel vulnerable or uncomfortable, you can either let it consume you, or you can choose to be grateful now that you have overcome it. It begins with a thought. The more you are able to transcend these negative emotions with constructive thoughts, the faster you will get past whatever made you feel so bad. Over time and with practice, the things you feared or felt bad about will dissolve away. So you keep on.

The next time a negative emotion arises, just say, "Thank you. I am so thankful now that this emotion no longer affects me. I chose to elevate my mood and keep getting better." Then you persist.

Let me leave you with this thought: I have experienced many people in life who ended up quitting various things. What I can conclude from people who start a thing but rarely finish it, is that: 1) They became so accustomed to quitting in life that it becomes a part of their paradigm (which, again, is a deep programming or conditioning of the mind); or 2) their desire was never as great as they claimed. If you are in either category, I am here to tell you that it's okay. If you fall into the first category it's not the end of the world, **but you can only change if you truly desire change**. Remember, the only person that can initiate or create change is you — not your parents, friends or relatives, boyfriend or girlfriend — it needs to come from within. You are free to choose what you want in this life. You create your destiny through what you constantly think and feel.

So if you're one who falls under the first category of people who constantly quit, "the cure", as so many people say, is to begin now to finish what you start. Begin with the little things if you have to. Sometimes, when I decide clean up around the house, I begin one chore but suddenly I become distracted by something completely different, telling myself, "ah, I can clean up later. My room isn't even all that bad." Guess what? Postponing cleaning my room lasts for weeks until I finally realize how messy it is. Often I'd do the same with the dishes when I was a kid. Clean a few, hear the doorbell ring, forget about the dishes and go outside and play. The mountain of dishes in the sink became flying saucers if my mom came back home before I did.

Keep in mind that whenever you stop (as stated in Murphy's bestseller The Power of Your Subconscious

<u>Mind</u>), you develop new grooves in your brain cells that impel your mind to believe it's okay to quit whatever you're doing. The more you do this, the more the habit is ingrained into your personality makeup. Reread this paragraph a few times, and the next time you think about quitting something (no matter how small), know that it is shaping your future because **we, as humans, are addicted to our habits**. You will come across a point in your life where quitting becomes easy and not only will you suffer, but those closest to you will as well.

On the other hand, you shouldn't continue doing something that makes you miserable. There is a distinct difference between that and quitting at the drop of a hat. When you feel that you are suffering for prolonged periods of time in a given situation, remember these words. I listened to them for the first time in a Bob Proctor Paradigm Shift seminar I purchased in 2018. Bob quotes a man named Robert Tew as saying, "Respect yourself enough to walk away from anything that no longer serves you, grows you, or makes you happy." The reason I want to leave this thought with you is because there are times (and this is crucial if you are a parent reading this) when a person no longer wants to play sports. Sometimes the love or drive for the game or competition just ends. Perhaps it was never there to begin with. There is nothing wrong with being honest with yourself. I think it is very important to get personal with you here because I can speak from experience. You will read later about how I saw with my very eyes the LoA work for me as a college athlete. The same chapter describes how exhilarating a certain experience was for me because my persistence was rewarded. But my love for the game was barely there throughout my last season playing football and I knew it was time for me to walk away.

After making my way up the depth chart at Phoenix College for the quarterback position, I realized something changed in how I felt about playing. Deep down I knew I was finished playing because practice had become a chore, I hated the feeling in my gut before games and I just wasn't happy playing anymore. It was no longer fun for me. I knew there were other things that I would rather be doing. Not wanting to give it half-effort, I made an extremely difficult decision.

As hard as it was, I walked away from football despite disappointing coaches and teammates who told me I couldn't just give up. I never saw it as quitting, and I never had any regrets. I am proud of my decision and walked away with my head held high knowing I'd had a good run. I will always love the game of football. It has brought me the greatest friends anyone could ever ask for, the greatest mentors and coaches, and numerous life lessons that I would probably not know otherwise. It taught me, first hand, that the Law of Attraction is real and it works in any walk of life — even sports. Had I chosen not to walk away when I did, you would probably not be reading this book.

There's a difference between walking away from something that no longer serves you and simply quitting simply because times get tough or because you simply don't want to put in the work. Not wanting to work hard for the thing desired, and suddenly stopping because you decide not to sacrifice, is real quitting. Know the difference.

If you happen to fall into the second category — which are those who quit because their desires are not as strong as they once thought — the simplest solution is to find something you really love to do, and dedicate your life to it. When you have found it, only then will you understand the meaning of persistence. Your passion to do this thing you set your mind to, regardless of circumstance, is what will allow you to push forward. As long as your desire to be the best is strong enough, persistence will be a true friend on your journey — a friend that will push against all obstacles to your success — no matter what. As Bob Proctor says, "Hold it in your mind and you will hold it in your hand." The Universe always molds itself into what you have faith in, persistence toward, and desire most.

When you have found something you love to do, you can not quit because your fire for the thing you love will see you through.

"Keep on keeping on, until the day breaks, and the shadows flee away."

— Joseph Murphy

SIX

Discipline – Stay Off the Ropes

STAY OFF THE ROPES! IF YOU'RE AN AVID FAN OF BOXING, I'm sure you've heard this term before. You hear the trainers from the corner screaming, "Off the ropes!" "Use the jab!" "Don't keep your head still!" "1-2 Combo, now!" As the fighters throw punches and dance around the ring, you can clearly see their energy decline in later rounds. Their movements are not nearly as smooth as they were before. As fatigue builds, you see their hands drop or their legs wobble. The trainer reminds them to stay **disciplined** even though their stamina seems to be waning.

Like the sound of thunder, boom! A right uppercut lands and sends one of the fighters stumbling into the ropes. He tries to regain his composure while his trainer is screaming, "Stay off the ropes, stay off the ropes!" Then comes a flurry of punches... left, right, jab, uppercut. "Hands up, protect yourself," yells the trainer. The opponent throws ferocious punches until a surprising right hook slips through, bringing the pain. Now he's hurt! A jab follows, then a right hook. A final left hook to the ribs and he hits the canvas. The ref counts to ten, and the fight is over. "What were you thinking?" the loser's trainer exclaims. Embarrassed and in pain, the loser sits dazed, still trying to figure out what just took place. When in reality, what happened was, the fighter who was rocked first stayed disciplined, and the fighter who lost did not.

You see this all the time in boxing. A fighter becomes overly-aggressive and leaves himself open to his opponent's counterpunch. Boxing champ, Floyd Mayweather, is known for taking advantage of such a situation. He understands that staying disciplined within his own mind (which his body will follow) is what will inevitably bring him victory. He is quoted as saying, "When you fight angry, you make a lot of mistakes, and when you fight a sharp, witty fighter like me, you can't make mistakes." Notice what he says about the angry, undisciplined fighter. He knows that when you aggravate negative emotion — which you are able to manage with enough practice — the opponent's doom is almost certain. Defeat waits to greet him with a smirk on its face, almost as if to say, "gotcha!" On the other hand, an angry but disciplined opponent would use his anger to fuel his victory.

Shannon Miller, the United States most decorated (16 medals) gymnast, was asked by Marjorie F. Eddington in an online interview to explain how discipline and a clear work ethic played a role in her success. She responded that had it not been for discipline, she would never have had the opportunity to compete in her first Olympics. That discipline, which took 10 years to develop, carried her to the top. Shannon says her coach still brags about her never missing practice. Not once — even if she was sick. How many times have you taken days off because your tummy hurt or because you had a headache? Real discipline is doing the things you know you need to do **even when you don't feel like it**. Think about what discipline does to a person. Yes, it hurts, but it will only make you stronger. Yes, it's tiring, but it will only make you more resilient. Yes, it's hard, but it creates persistence. How great is the prize of discipline when we overlook all the "I don't want to's!"

If you are discouraged because of a situation in your sport, hang tight. Your discipline, plus your positive mindset, will help you to get over that hump. I have said it over and over and I will continue to do so hoping these words will be implanted in your subconscious: Whatever you desire to manifest, **will**. Always keep your prize before you and continue to do the things you need to. If that means going to sleep early so you can wake up early each and every day, then so be it. If that means denying yourself a pack of Oreos, then that's what you need to do. If that means meditating for 20 minutes, then do it. Discipline is about taking every step in the right direction, and then reaping the reward with a smile on your face.

When you think about what discipline means, one of the most important things to take from it is the ability to be prepared. Hall of Famer for the National Hockey League, Wayne Gretzky, in a video interview with NowThisNews, said he knew stats for every single player in the league at the time. He watched games every night to ensure that he was prepared for his opponents. Discipline is doing the physical, mental, emotional, and spiritual work that needs to be done — even if you don't want to do it. That is true commitment. Former college football player and now renowned public speaker, Inky Johnson said, "Commitment is staying true to what you said you would do long after the mood you said it in has left." Staying committed to one's discipline is everything because it develops not only the skills necessary to improve, but it builds character. "Sweat-equity," as Inky calls it, builds you up and restrains you from quitting because of all the work you have put in.

One last example of the importance of discipline is in the words of the NFL's greatest wide receiver Jerry Rice, also interviewed by NowThisNews. According to Rice, perhaps the best term to describe his legacy is **work ethic**. It is no accident that the league's greatest receiver outworked every opponent he faced, which propelled him to become a hall of famer and break practically every wide receiver record in the NFL.

And finally, as this book is not designed to give you a workout regimen to follow or specific exercises for certain muscle groups. This is designed to help you realize that it **all** starts in your mind. **If** you truly desire to be disciplined, there is an infinite amount of resources you can use to improve at your particular sport or competition. There is no excuse. Remember, "When you want something, all the Universe conspires in helping you to achieve it." You will find the right people, because they will be attracted to you. The same goes for any article, workout program, or mentor you will ever need. Be vigilant, and keep an open mind about what comes your way. Whenever you receive what you have been looking for, remind yourself that God or the Universe may have just winked at you.

SEVEN

The Dark Side

STAR WARS HAS ALWAYS BEEN ONE OF MY FAVORITE MOVIE series. The lightsaber battles, the spaceships, and the intergalactic travels all seemed designed to blow my mind. My favorite character was Darth Maul because he had a double-sided lightsaber. I remember constantly reenacting the ending scene of Episode I - The Phantom Menace wherein, Darth Maul fights Qui-Gon Jinn and Obi-Wan Kenobi. I was, of course, Darth Maul. The fact that he got sliced in half never mattered to me, because at seven years old, he was my favorite villain of all time. Something about the devilish look in his eyes captivated me. His quiet, yet sinister attitude was mesmerizing. Isn't it interesting how we as humans are so drawn to the unpleasant? Why is it that we linger around, waiting to see what adverse things lurk around the corner? Our thoughts often ponder upon the underside of life. We often even fantasize about unfortunate events that may happen to us or those we know.

Think back. Have you ever thought negatively about a situation and your imagination just ran wild? Thought after thought, you pile on more of the same ideas alike to the original thought. After some time — yet before you know it — you've run through 15 different scenarios about that situation, giving rise to fear, anger, frustration, jealousy, and rage. There you are now in your own little world, surrounded by all of these detrimental emotions in your mind! Now your body joins in on what you think and your hands start getting clammy, your heart rate increases, blood pressure increases and you start making those faces like you just smelled some crap. This is because, as previously stated, **your body always follows your mind.** Isn't it funny though, how this all began with a single idea?

I chose Star Wars as a theme because even Yoda, the legendary Jedi Master, knows a thing or two about the Law of Attraction. Okay, okay, maybe not. But "The Force" he always talks about, has many similarities to how our energy affects our destiny.

In watching The Phantom Menace again recently, I had forgotten all about the little, wise, green creature when he said, "Fear is the path to the dark side. Fear leads to anger, anger leads to hate. Hate leads to suffering." Yoda understood that you begin running in circles once you entertain a negative emotion. And what have we been saying all along about these internal states of feeling and being? That the more you focus on these emotions, the more you will attract circumstances in harmony with anger, fear, frustration, etc. in your life. Energy flows, where attention goes! Dr. Joe Dispenza says, "What you put your attention on and mentally rehearse over and over again not only becomes who you are from a biological perspective, it also determines your future." Why? Because your body cannot tell the difference between what is real and what is imagined. And since the body always follows the mind, it would make sense that the more you think of failure or frustration, the more it will show up in your future of playing/competing. This may be one of the main reasons why many athletes get stuck in what we call "slumps". The repeated thoughts of fear, failure, frustration, envy, jealousy, or complacency condition one to live sulked in past emotions which forces an athlete to repeat the same reality in his/her future.

Johnny Bench, Hall of Fame catcher for the Major League Baseball's Cincinnati Reds says, "Slumps are like a soft bed. They're easy to get into and hard to get out of." Since we are creatures of habit, it would make sense then that our addiction to our daily patterns of thinking, speaking, and doing, trap us into living the same life every single day. It is not until we realize this pattern and intentionally work to get out of it, that we are able to break out and finally become whatever it is we dream of.

Your continuous actions, thoughts, habits — whatever you want to point out — are all some sort of conditioning that you have acquired since a very young age. For most people reading this book, the principles outlined may seem very fine and dandy on paper, but it will be extremely hard to break out of the paradigms you have been accustomed to **since birth**. Proctor explains that from the moment you take your first breath, your subconscious mind is retaining all information given to it. If your environment was filled with anger, guilt, fear, or anxiety, it is most likely that you are conditioned to be the same. The repetition of information presented to you — whether you realize it or not — was probably one of the strongest influences on the person you are at this very moment. So if you have deep-rooted issues due to lack of love, security, etc. in your childhood, know that it's not your fault. You have been dealt a hand wherein you had no control. You can't change the past. What **is** in your control is what **you decide** to do with it. If you believe the information in this book is true (and you will definitely come to believe if you do some deep self-analysis) then you can no longer point the finger at anyone but yourself. When you analyze yourself deeply, you will realize that **you have attracted everything — good and bad in your life.** Yes, in some way shape or form, you have attracted that loss, that game-winning shot, that knockdown you took, those missed shots, the cut, the scholarship… **You** did it.

I understand that some of you may feel pretty upset or even angry about what you just read. But it's true. And here is the bottom line. Those beliefs, the programming you have received since birth, have been passed on through countless generations. What we think about life, how we are supposed to live versus how we **are** living is the result of previous and sometimes ignorant and misguided values. Now you might be losing it. "You're crazy! Do you really mean to tell me that I brought my sickness, my injury, or my failure at sports upon myself?" I will answer your question with several questions. Do you believe that you are a limited being? Do you find sickness and misery normal? Do you honestly believe that the world is only getting worse and worse? Do you really think that because you "sin", God is going to punish you unless you repent 100,000 times? Or do you believe that there is a power outside of yourself (a negative one at that) which is out to "…steal and kill and destroy" *(John 10:10)*. Do you think you are vulnerable to this "devil" or evil?

If you believe these things which have been passed

down to you, you will find them in your experience. Not only will you find them, you will be looking for them to prove that the things you believe are true. These ideas, concepts, or beliefs are emotionalized because you've been fed these things your entire life so they have become a part of your faith. Therefore, it would make sense to say *"We don't see things as they are, we see them as we are."* — *Anaïs Nin, French-Cuban American diarist.*

I can't tell you exactly why children die. I cannot explain why you were born with a disability. The beliefs we hold, what we have been told our entire lives, have more power than we could ever imagine. Most of these beliefs are subtle and hidden within our subconscious depths, which explains why it can be so hard to change the way we think and feel about a situation. But once you are able to transcend these lies, you will notice your life begin to change. Trust us when we tell you we've been there. Once we changed our energy (the way we think and feel), we were able to change our destiny. It is the reason we were able to write this book, and it is the reason you will know to make the change for yourself, to live a life not in fear, misery, or poverty, but in love, peace, joy, and triumph.

After you recognize that you are the creator of your universe and there is nothing left to chance, accepted the fact that **you control your destiny** and in your hands and mind is all the power you need to be anything you want, your life will begin to turn around. What's done is done, lose the guilt. Forgive yourself and know that it's okay. It's never too late to change your thoughts and focus your energy forward.

The time to turn things around is now. Break the habits — the negative ones you're addicted to — and become a new being. Decide in this moment to become the person you dream of. Then, create a clear picture in your mind, walk in the light of this new person. Walk as if the stars, the sun, the moon, the clouds and the trees and every living and nonliving particle of energy is on your side. When you begin to feel invincible, you will become it. Earl Nightingale said it best, "We become what we think about."

So you may be asking, "What does any of this have to do with sports? How does leaving behind negative emotions, the conditioning of my upbringing, the changing of my character, etc… How is any of this relevant to what I am trying to accomplish?" **It is everything**! What we are up to here is getting you to realize that any negative thoughts emotionalized will only impede your progress in sports until you learn to transmute that energy into something positive. When negative energy presents itself (which it will), you must learn to transform it into something beneficial. Or, you could ignore the negative thought altogether because remember, a thought has no power unless it becomes emotionalized. Learn to dismiss those thoughts or use them as fuel to build a fire within.

Uncontrolled emotions are what will hurt you. Anger, when out of control clouds an athlete's mind and takes his focus off the task at hand. Nervousness, when you allow it to consume you, can turn into fear, which can only lead to mistakes. Eventually, you'll learn to use your anger as strength, and your nervousness as excitement. You get the idea. It is crucial that you learn to discipline your mind. If you don't, **your mind will fall and your body will follow**. The automatic processes involved in everyday function will take over your mind to the point where you think, act, and feel as you did before. By the end of this book, you will have

49

GILBERT VILLALOBOS & ALBERTO FLORES

a better idea of how to change your destructive habits into constructive ones.

If you want to change your current reality, you must learn to stop living by the programs of your past and train your mind to live in the future that you desire. "Think of the thing desired, and feel its reality now!" (Joseph Murphy, The Power of Your Subconscious Mind)

When I was pitching at Cal State Northridge, I went through a period of time in which I became extremely envious of the starting pitchers. I saw them out on the mound while I was in the dugout and thought to myself, "I hope this dude gets a homer hit off him. I hope this guy walks everyone he throws against." I said all of this not realizing that I was attracting negativity to myself by emotionalizing my negative energy. Guess what happened when I hit the mound. I would walk guys and players would get hits off me. They were all around bad outings. It was all because the negative energy I was placing (or I thought I was placing) on others, was coming back and kicking my own butt.

The negativity that I applied in this situation made bad things come back to me. This is why it's so important to be grateful and positive about what you are doing. Even though I rooted for my team, I never fully gave in to wishing the good for those other pitchers ahead of me. You cannot fool the Universe, as it always returns your energy in like kind. So you understand how important it is to be mindful of how you are thinking and feeling.

If you don't believe what is being said, then you can try this for yourself. Take it from me and learn from my mistakes, or fall into the trap yourself and see just how fast negativity halts your success.

The continuous and repetitive information that you allow to linger in your brain will eventually become who you are. Since you become addicted to your thoughts and feelings, keep them high and positive as your reality is a reflection of them. In the next chapter, you will discover the importance of great words when fused with intense feeling. This is one of the ways you can elevate your energy to be more in line with what you want and avoid the famous player's slump. And could you believe this "slump" is not even real? Read that sentence again and let it marinate. It only exists in your mind. The faster you recognize this, the faster you will get back on track.

Whenever you're off your game, one of the best things you can do is detach from whatever you're doing. If you continue to work on your craft with this bad energy, you will remain stagnated. Take an hour, a day, a week, whatever time you need to clear your head and return with **elevated** positive emotions rather than negative feelings such as frustration or inadequacy.

In an interview with my friend Muhammad Oliver, former NFL Denver Bronco, he said one of the best things to do when you're struggling in sports is to get back to basics and trust your coaching. Take a step back, take a deep breath, and know everything is going to be okay. Time is not running out. As long as you believe that this break will benefit you, it will. Relax, you are exactly where you need to be. You will receive everything necessary for the realization of your dreams. If you can bring yourself to believe that every thing that happens in your life works out for your good, it will be so.

Too many times, negative energy arises in our hearts and minds because we trust our physical senses way more than trusting our deeper — and vastly superior — mind. Perhaps the main reason for this is because our five senses remind us of our current circumstances. If you can remain disciplined with the work you have done with your mind, regardless of matter, you are sure to meet victory. However, if you are constantly checking your rankings and don't see yourself moving up, you are only affirming your senses, which signal a message in your brain that maybe you aren't that great — that this is where you belong and you'll never get over that hump. Here is where frustration, rage, envy, and other negative emotions arise. If we can just learn to trust that the images held in our minds **with expectancy** will materialize, there are no limits to what we can do!

And here is the turning point. Are you ready for it? The negative energy you're holding on to can be converted into that magical stuff called triumph. Most of the elites, people like Michael Jordan, Mike Tyson, Floyd Mayweather, Tom Brady, and many more, have talked about how the criticisms of others have always driven them to be better. They use all that talk to fuel their fire. How is this even possible? Because of this little gift called **perception**. The only difference between what you consider "good" and what you consider "bad" is how you choose to look at the situation.

When you think about death, do you consider it something negative or positive? My guess is you'd say, "negative," right? Well, what if a police officer shot and killed a terrorist before he could murder 20 innocent people? Your answer might change. You see, it all depends on **how** you look at the situation. Perception allows us to change how we view something negative just enough for it to benefit our lives. That is the "secret" of transmuting something negative to something positive. Just change your thoughts about that thing.

So the next time you are faced with adversity, think of it as a gift. Whenever you are told you are not good enough, be grateful for the fact that you are about to prove these people wrong. Whenever you feel fear or doubt, know that your solution is on the opposite side of the same spectrum — faith and confidence. When you face an opponent bigger, faster, stronger than you, be grateful that you are about to show the world something spectacular.

Your greatest enemy is fear. Like Phil told me, "Fear gets you hurt." It leaves you in shame. It's what stops so many people from ever doing any of the things they love because it keeps them in a shell. When you let fear slow you down, you become another statistic. Ask yourself, what is really stopping me from making that play? What is stopping me from defeating the person in front of me? Is it my lack of skill? Or is it that I am afraid? Remember the wise words of Yoda the next time you're facing fear. "...Fear leads to anger, anger leads to hate, hate leads to suffering." Don't tolerate being in that state for even a second!

Fear comes knocking at everyone's door, but the most efficient repellent is faith. What is faith? Faith is belief in a thought, concept, or idea. True faith, can bring you closer to the realization of your heart's desires.

"He who has overcome his fears, will truly be free"

— *Aristotle*

EIGHT

Affirmations/Incantations — "I am vs. I AM!"

Proverbs 15:4 Kind words bring life, but cruel words crush your spirit.

"Words have the power to both destroy and heal. When words are both true and kind, they can change our world."

— Buddha

"I AM" IS THE MAIN TOPIC OF THIS CHAPTER. THERE IS SO much power behind these words, and when we finish the sentence, we become that which we say. As you know, conversations with yourself or with others about yourself are more powerful than you could ever grasp. When you emotionalize these words, you add energy to what you speak. And since everything is energy, that means that our thoughts go some place, and if you take time to reflect, you will definitely see that your energy always returns back to you. That is the LoA at work. So what about these "I am" statements is so important? They are messages you send out to the irrefutable LoA which brings to fruition what you affirm about yourself.

Murphy explains further in his book, The Power of Your Subconscious Mind. If your subconscious mind picks up all information fed to it, then the words it hears (this includes talks with yourself) will be accepted by it, unless we reject them. Once accepted, your subconscious mind carries out the order or belief given to it, good or bad. But, it's important to know that a positive thought is stronger than your negative ones.

So if I say to myself, **with feeling**, "I am so happy and grateful," my mind and body would not only see to it that I feel happy and grateful, but would also begin to muster similar thoughts and emotions to make me feel so. Just as a negative thought, once emotionalized, generates countless ways to see "the bad", so will a positive thought or statement find numerous expressions in harmony with the original thought or statement. This cycle of positive energy begins to align you with your desire and the more positive emotions involved, the more of them you will attract in your life. Here is where the magic begins. Your affirmation — statement or proposition declared to be true — is pressed into your subconscious, and the more it is emotionalized, the more it makes an impression in the brain cells, producing a stronger connection in your mind. If repeated enough times, with enough energy, you'll come to believe what you're saying. The key here is to teach your subconscious to accept the thought. And since your unconscious mind speaks a language of images and metaphors, you must learn to visualize the end result of what you desire!

. . .

I AM sure you have come across some version of this statement in your life. It goes like this, 'Watch your thoughts, they become words; watch your words, they become actions; watch your actions, they become habits; watch your habits, they become character; watch your character, for it becomes your destiny.' [Author unknown] This quote confirms each and every thing we have been talking about from the moment you opened this book. When you affirm a thought to yourself over and over again, you will eventually come to believe it. And since belief in a thought or idea is faith, your faith will carry you wherever you go. This is why your affirmations must be used to help and not harm you. Watch your thoughts!

Now let's take it up a notch. Here is where we learn to take our affirmations to the next level, what motivational speaker Tony Robbins calls 'incantations'. Affirmations are stepping stones to incantations which raise your physical, mental, and spiritual energy. They're like affirmations on steroids.

As we get into what you desire in sports, you must be clear about your intentions. And once you identify that intention, proclaim to the Universe with every fiber of your being that it's already yours. For example, I got the beginning of all my affirmations from Bob Proctor. "I am so happy and grateful that..." and **you** fill in the blank. Want to get faster? Want to throw harder or be more accurate? Want to lift more weight? The power is all in your thoughts and words **magnified by your body's actions.** The more energy you put into your words, the more they become real. Use as much of your body as you can when repeating your incantations which need to become so much a part of you that they are engrained in your nervous system. Shout them out loud! Jump, scream, beat your chest, and feel it deep in your gut — what you are affirming **is you**!

MOST PROFESSIONAL ATHLETES have a lot of practice with affirmations without realizing. Since it is also known as auto-suggestion (or suggesting something specific to oneself), if you pay close attention, they all have nothing but great (and true) things to say about themselves. That is what having a "winner's mentality" is all about — thinking only of the desired result. Watch interviews or press conferences with the best. Some are extremely outspoken about how great their talents are, while others are more humble and reserved. But don't get it twisted, a show of humility doesn't mean they're about to roll all over you and embarrass you in front of everybody. Their quiet confidence, their internal conversations is what allows this to happen. While studying the greatest to ever play sports, I have never come across an interview or press conference in where the athlete doubted his ability. I've never seen an elite player talk about how weak he is or that he doesn't believe in himself.

Take a step back and look at yourself in the mirror. How many times have your negative thoughts about yourself hurt you? Or how many times have you set yourself up for failure by simply saying something negative about yourself? As soon as you fall into the trap of internalizing negative energy, you have lost. The LoA doesn't doesn't care who you are! Since your body always follows your mind, doesn't it make sense that as soon as you think of failure, you inevitably attract it? If you think to yourself, "**Don't** screw this up, don't screw this up" then because energy flows where focus goes, you'll do just that!

At the same time you're working your butt off, if you continue to repeat with feeling, over and over and over again, "I am so happy and grateful now, that I am improving on my 100 meter time every day," you'll get just that in your experience. Of course, this comes with time, and a lot of practice. Don't expect to become the world's greatest lifter after you've affirmed to yourself in one day that you are. No, work is required for this process. What I'm getting at here is demanding your subconscious mind to accept the idea you are presenting it so that once it is anchored in you, the rest will flow. After all the practice, after you've done everything necessary in pursuit of your goal, your incantations will allow your subconscious (your body) to bring the rest to you. Since energy follows focus, you will invariably manifest your desires.

So remember, "I am" holds all the power. Start now, (even if you've gone your whole life believing what everyone else tells you and have given in to their negative suggestions) talk only about the things you desire. Begin to speak words of power, gratitude, authority, courage, and faith. When you have said it enough times, with enough feeling, you will become your words. Old Earl said it best. "We become what we think about."

Once you have taken time to speak those words of power over your sports career (which you should be repeating aloud with the greatest intensity about 10 million times a day), you will begin to feel with your mind soul and body what you are stating is true, and the faster you will come to receive your reward.

Dispenza says when we change our energy, we change

our physical state. This means that we prepare our minds and bodies for an event that has yet to take place, but will. Once we are in this high state of vibration (with emotions of love, gratitude, joy, freedom, and faith), what we attract into our lives will match that frequency. This is why incantations are so effective! They prime you for the outcome in advance. God, the Universe, Higher Power, whatever you want to call it, will respond to your elevated thought. Every thing we put out will return to us; there is no getting around it.

To wrap up this chapter, let's take a look at one of the best UFC fighters of this era. If you do not know who Jon "Bones" Jones is, you are definitely missing out on some serious action. Except for one disqualification in December 2009, Jones has a perfect record in the octagon. You can find a video on YouTube if you search "Jon Jones Law of Attraction" that shows how a person who knows about the LoA can utilize it to reach the pinnacle of their career. In this video, he says he always follows an autograph with "Champion 2011". He goes on to say, "I believe in the Law of Attraction, and I believe that you can speak things into existence. And I believe that when you know where you're going and you know what you want, the Universe has a way of stepping aside for you..." Wow! It doesn't get clearer than this. It all begins in your mind, and the Universe will mold itself to give you exactly what you want after you begin to demand it. Not from a place of weakness, but with strength, passion, love, and power.

NINE

Gratitude

I KNOW WHAT YOU'RE THINKING, "WHAT IN THE HECK does gratitude have to do with my success in sports?" Everything! Why? Because gratitude is the number one ingredient that you need to reach your potential. Yeah, this may sound far-fetched, but let me explain. There is a saying that goes like this, "If you're not grateful for what you have now, you'll never reach what you've set out to be." Why? Because some circumstance, some "slump", some adversity will meet you on your journey, and there must be a way to get you through it. The one thing that not only allows you to push through, but gets you on "the other side" without feeling empty or frustrated, is gratitude. Whenever you are able to focus your attention on a problem, and then turn it into something good, and find some way or reason to be grateful for it, you are not only strengthening your ability to perceive things differently, but you are putting out a signal to God or the Universe that will infallibly return to you what you feel and in equal amounts. The moment you turn your situation into something worse than it is, you begin to add more of that negative energy to your life.

I know how easy it is to trigger a negative thought. As hard as you may try, the thought lingers and lingers until it consumes your whole being. These cases are natural, as there is always something that can cause you to feel rage, resentment, shame, or failure. At times, there is no way around this. What is most important here is that you **choose** to move into an elevated emotion. Think to yourself, "How can I use this to help me?" "What can I learn from this?" If we can choose to see our obstacles as something to help us evolve, there is nothing that can defeat us.

One of the main reasons gratitude is mentioned in this book; and the reason it is so important is because this elevated emotion (like others such as love, confidence, and faith) creates something called "heart coherence." This discovery from HeartMath Institute shows how maintaining an elevated emotion keeps a coherent signal or relationship between the brain and the heart. When your heart and brain are in coherence, you are able to perform at a higher level. The article below from HeartMath Institute explains why.

HEARTMATH RESEARCH DEMONSTRATES that different patterns of heart activity (which accompany different emotional states) have distinct effects on cognitive and emotional function. During stress and negative emotions, when the heart rhythm pattern is erratic and disordered, the corresponding pattern of neural signals traveling from the heart to the brain inhibits higher cognitive functions. This limits our ability to think clearly, remember, learn, reason, and make effective decisions. (This helps explain why we may often act impulsively and unwisely when we're under stress.)

The heart's input to the brain during stressful or negative emotions also has a profound effect on the brain's emotional processes — actually serving to reinforce the emotional experience of stress.

In contrast, the more ordered and stable pattern of the heart's input to the brain during positive emotional states has the opposite effect – it facilitates cognitive function and reinforces positive feelings and emotional stability. This means that learning to generate increased heart rhythm coherence, by sustaining positive emotions, not only benefits the entire body, but also profoundly affects how we perceive, think, feel, and perform.

WHEN YOU ARE under a lot of stress (also known as a negative state) while playing or competing, you tend to make more mistakes. This is just one reason to be grateful. Aside from affecting performance, gratitude for something in advance speeds up the process even more toward what you desire. If you are at a practice and constantly complain about the heat, the mud, the atmosphere, or your teammate(s), you are placing your energy on something outside of yourself. Dispenza says it very clearly, "When you give your energy to the external environment, there's no room for any creative energy within you to flow." This can cause you to feel blocked. When you hit that wall ahead, it'll be extremely difficult to get over it because there is nothing positive to keep you pushing forward. Remember, your thoughts return to you in their physical equivalent. Your biology changes, your environment changes, your destiny changes. As long as you persist with your positive emotions, your Universe will mold to become what you want.

Let's put this into perspective. If you happen to be in a weightlifting competition and perform so poorly your day is done, there are many things you can do. There are three options. You can 1) choose to mope and complain about everything that went wrong at the competition and think about how bad you sucked, or 2) you can use negativity to fight your way to improvement, or 3) you can immediately reflect on the positives, be grateful for them, and then work even harder towards your goal with a positive vibration. I hope with my whole heart that you are able to recognize by now how detrimental the first choice is. It not only keeps you down for a longer time, it attracts more negative thoughts, feelings, and circumstances to you. This condition will continue recurring until you change your mindset. The second option is slightly better than option one because you're taking some type of action toward your goal, but you're still in a negative vibration. But let's analyze the third option. This can produce miracles in your life. You leave the competition knowing you could have done much better, even feeling like you failed. But you realize that negative thoughts only create negative energy so you choose to instead look at something good about the event. Aha! Here is something… "Well, I didn't perform like I wanted to, but that's okay. There are still positives." "Well," you might think, "I've come a long way from where I first started. I've worked so hard to even get here. That's something to be grateful about." Here is where your momentum begins! It all starts with an idea in your mind. Nothing changed about the competition, the only thing that has changed now, is how you choose to perceive what happened. "What else is there to be grateful for? Well, I'm thankful to even have the opportunity to to do this. I know there are a lot of people that don't ever get the chance." Now we are cooking! "There is a lot I need to improve on, and I'm glad my friends and family are always there to help me with whatever I need. My coaches, too. They're definitely the best. But most of all, I'm grateful that my time is coming. All of my hard work, all that I have worked so hard for, **will** pay off. I know it because I have the drive, the right people in my corner, and belief in my own abilities. I **will** get this!"

Take a look at what has happened. You have taken your focus and energy off of what you don't want to continue in your life with a single, sincere thought and become elevated in your emotions by visualizing and pondering all that you desire. It becomes a domino effect and before you know it, you will become grateful for even the loss. Your performance, that seemed so bad, will only serve now to make you better. You learn the most from losses (**if you choose to**) because they allow you to make the necessary adjustments to evolve as a human being and an athlete.

Notice that the third option propels you to view things from a different light and allows you to become grateful for what's seemingly bad.

Here is an exercise you can try for yourself, anywhere, any time. I learned this at a 2018 Tony Robbins seminar. First, place your hands on your heart, and all of your focus to that area with as much love, gratitude, and joy as you can. Visualize energy flowing to your heart and the area surrounding it. You will notice your emotions instantly elevate. I've always felt warmth deep within. Now take a minute each to think of three things you're grateful for (three minutes total). Afterwards, your breathing and heart rate will slow down and you'll feel more relaxed, thinking more clearly than before this exercise. In this beautiful state, take the energy to your heart, and think of three more things you are grateful for that have **not** happened yet (but as you know by now, they will materialize through the principles outlined in this book) as though what you are feeling grateful for has happened already.

If you have trouble feeling as if what you're grateful for has already happened, think about this for a moment. Pretend you asked a relative for a new phone for Christmas and they told you that they would get it for you. How would you feel in that instant? I'm sure you'd feel great, right? You could, in that moment, already feel grateful for what you know is to come. When Christmas rolls around, you are in a state of expectancy and what you asked for is presented. That is what it's all about. This is why Jesus said, "Therefore I tell you, whatever you ask for in prayer, believe that you have received it, and it will be yours" *(Mark 11:24 NIV)*. The only difference between the exercise and the Christmas present is that most times you **don't know** exactly when your desire will materialize. **All you know is that it will**. That is faith.

Back to the exercise... When you see in your mind's eye what you want to experience, remember from the chapter on visualization that the more detailed the image and the more feeling involved, the stronger the frequency that you send out. The more you are able to visualize (and you will get better with practice) the more quickly your dream will come knocking at your door — with work. I want to emphasize that your thoughts and feelings alone will not bring about the result. But if your thoughts actually manifest, your drive to create a physical experience will become greater since your thoughts drive your body into action. When your desire is strong enough, the work isn't really "work" at all. It becomes something that you love to do. When you love what you do (which produces an elevated emotion), you not only increase energy, but what you seek comes to you faster than you could ever imagine.

All we are is a human tuning fork. In an experiment conducted by Massachusetts Institute of Technology, scientists demonstrated how tuning forks "tap" into the same frequency. If you were to hit a tuning fork next to another one of the same size, weight, and shape, the tuning fork that was not touched would begin to vibrate and make sound just the same as the one that was unattended. Now, if you placed a weight on the second tuning fork, and left the first tuning fork the same and hit it, the second fork would not vibrate or make sound because it would not be on the same frequency. Now, if you placed a weight on both forks, they would both make sound after only one of them was tapped because they're vibrating on the same frequency. It is the same with us! Our minds, our hearts, our bodies, are tuning forks. Our level of vibration (or frequency) is what determines what we bring into our experience. It doesn't get more simple than this.

If we could only understand that our vibration determines our reality, we would be much more careful about what we feed our brains. If we could all be more cognizant of the conversations we have with ourselves, what we choose to accept as true (whether through the suggestions given by others or ourselves) we would save ourselves a load of trouble. And we would begin to live a more beautiful life. It's simple. The reason so many of us don't do it is because we trust our conscious mind more than our subconscious. What qualities or attributes make up our subconscious? All of the unknowns: vibration, energy, love, peace and any other beautiful thing not visible to the eye. Gratitude makes us feel better and allows us to see the beauty in everything, even our problems. You are exactly where you need to be. You are in the perfect spot. Believe and be grateful for that. Believe and be grateful that every thing thing works out for your good, no matter how bad things may seem. You are chosen, you are special. There is absolutely no one else on the planet that can compete like you, that can run like you, can jump, or swing, or throw, or lift like you can. You do it special because you do it like no one else on this planet can.

Choose to be grateful right now, in this instant, and watch the magic happen before your eyes.

I am so happy and grateful now, *that everyday, in every way, I'm getting better and better!*

— Emile Coue, French psychologist

TEN

Patience – Trust the Process

"So be patient with gracious patience."

- The Holy Quran 70:05 (Surah Al-Ma'Arij)

YOU'VE HEARD SINCE CHILDHOOD THAT GOOD THINGS come to those who wait. There is some truth to that statement. **Good things come to those who wait because they have done their part for the fulfillment of their desires, and placed their energy and trust in what they know will inevitably come to pass.** It's trusting that the Universe will take care of everything you need in order for your dream to transform into reality.

Patience in athletes is essential to allow for development of the mind, body, and spirit. Every resource and opportunity you need will come to you, but the key is mastering patience. Now, don't get me wrong, I am not saying that only visualizing, having faith and expectancy, and mastering patience will bring to you the things you want out of your sports career. **Results require action.** As this book is about guiding you to use your mind constructively, understand that nothing worth having ever comes easy. **You must be willing to put in the work.** To be great, the grind is **always** necessary.

What makes patience such an asset (after your mind is programmed to see it this way) is finding the beauty of the present moment. After all of the practicing, studying, exercising, etc., you will come to love and enjoy every step along the way to realizing your dream. And yes, even the hard work.

Without the art of patience, you will not go far. Muhammad Oliver, an old friend and former NFL defensive back for the Denver Broncos once told me, "Patience is critical for long-term success because it allows you to grow and learn everything you need to in order to be the best at what you're doing." Remember that just because you desire something doesn't mean you'll receive it with a snap of your finger. The manifestation of what you desire is already coming. All you need to do is wait with faith and expectancy, and it **will** come to you. **Have the mentality that there is no way that it can't. It must.** Once you understand that manifestations are simply a reflection of your energy (how you think and feel on a minute-to-minute basis), you will be certain that what you seek, is already on its way to you.

Napoleon Hill said, "You cannot get something for nothing." Translation: there is no free lunch! Be willing to put in the time, the work, the studying, the meditating and everything else necessary to realize what you desire.

Take a step back and really think. Ask yourself this question and be honest about the answer: 'Am I really ready for what's next?' Are you?

Whether you are transitioning from 7th to 8th grade, or on your way to play college ball or the pros, are you ready for the next level? Have you learned what's necessary for the progression of your sports career? **If you cannot be patient for the things you desire, you will never develop the tools to become what you want.** Have you practiced enough that your movements are 'second nature'? Are you disciplined enough to block the negative remarks from the stands? The time needed to master such skills is vital.

In a study conducted by Stanford University back in the 1970s, a group of four-year-olds were placed in separate rooms and asked to sit down. A marshmallow was placed in front of each of them on a table. Then they were told that if they could wait until the conductor returned — which was 15 minutes — they would receive not one, but two marshmallows to eat. Imagine how antsy most of these children were! Many squirmed, bit their nails, and sniffed the marshmallow until it was practically up their nose, while others stared for what seemed to them a millennium. The results concluded that only 1 out of 3 children were patient and disciplined enough to wait until the conductor came back. What is even more interesting is that these children were followed throughout their lifetimes and were found to be more successful than the children who rushed to eat the single marshmallow. The successful children, at such a young age, knew the importance of **delayed gratification** i.e., which is resisting an impulse for an immediate reward in the hope of obtaining a more valued reward in the future (britannica.com). This experiment became very popular over the years and is now well-known as the Marshmallow Test. You can find videos of it on YouTube, and TED

Talks has a video as well if you'd like to check it out. The experiment demonstrates how important it is to wait. As previously mentioned, my great friend, Phil Bates, admitted to me that had he been more patient throughout his NFL career, had he mastered the art of waiting with faith and expectancy, he believes he would still be playing in the league. His impatience caused him to make impulsive decisions which put a halt to his career and forced him to retire. Let this be a learning experience from someone who made it to the top.

When you think in terms of the Law of Attraction, patience is crucial for success because it allows everything to manifest the perfect way and in the time best suited for **you**. No two people have the same situation, no two people are alike. What will manifest for you, and how it will manifest will be different than how it has for your friends and family. I'll give you a quick example. When I earned the opportunity to play quarterback at Phoenix College, I came in as the 3rd string. Being only 5'9, I knew I would be overlooked (literally). I knew I would have to prove myself both physically and mentally. Luckily, one of the things I understood about my situation was that my current status didn't matter, it was my thoughts and feelings that would dictate my reality. You must understand that even when you learn and prove for yourself just how powerful your mind is, there are still times when you will feel as though you are having a relapse. Its okay! It happened to me! I will never forget one of my phone calls with my coach when he told me about a "mindshift" he made wherein his whole life changed drastically for the better. Not knowing what this "mindshift" was, I asked him to explain it and what he was doing that was so life-changing. His answer was, "All you need to do, is feel as if what you want has already happened. Say, 'I am so happy and grateful that... and you fill in the blank.'"

After this phone call, I decided to try it. I began to affirm, "I am so happy and grateful now that I love football and I have so much fun playing it!" "I am so happy and grateful now, that I love football, and I have so much fun playing it!" I repeated this to myself every single chance that I got. I repeated it with feeling and I felt what I would feel it had already happened. What I had really desired, was to become the starting quarterback at Phoenix College. I didn't need to state that though, because my subconscious already knew exactly what I wanted. I repeated this affirmation until it became an incantation. I poured so much love, excitement, and feeling into it that I would be in my car on my way to school screaming at the top of my lungs, "I am so happy and grateful now, that I love football, and I have so much fun playing it!" Of course, I'd find myself looking to my right and left at times to discover some person staring at me like I was a maniac. But that was okay, **I was willing to do whatever it took to get what I wanted**. I kept this up for about 2-3 months.

Can you guess what began to happen? Little by little, things started turning around in my favor. The two quarterbacks in front of me kept making mistakes and I kept getting better. The most challenging part about this situation was not allowing myself to feel jealousy towards these two guys because they always took more reps than I did. I think for many athletes, one of the main reasons they never get the opportunity they are looking for is because they let jealousy disrupt what is already manifesting for them. Why? Because jealousy detracts from what you want! You may not realize it, but your jealous feelings breed more jealousy, like a snowball rolling down a mountain, further delaying your desires. The longer you stay in that negative state, the more time it will take for your dream to manifest. If you keep that bad energy long enough, it will only be a matter of time before all of your opportunities fly away. Your jealousy only ends up hurting you in the end.

Now back to what my story. I kept waiting, knowing my opportunity was right around the corner. By the third game, neither of the other two quarterbacks produced any results and my name was called. I had never been more ready for anything in my life. My first college career drive, and I drove down the field 70 yards for a touchdown. The emotions and excitement I felt were indescribable. I will never forget that moment because I was reminded that **I had already felt it months previous!** In that instant, I proved to myself, that the LoA is real, that my energy really did create my reality. Regardless of any circumstance, I knew and felt in my heart that **it would happen because I felt and believed it would happen.** I experienced the LoA right before my eyes. All of the visualization, the waiting, the practicing, had paid off and when I leaped in the air to celebrate the touchdown, it was as if the Universe itself came to my embrace and whispered, "This is only the beginning." Electricity and energy, fire and passion, and love and joy all came at once to greet me. I knew right then and there that thoughts become things.

Another prime example of patience can be seen in pro sports drafts. Isn't it crazy how some of the greatest athletes of all time have been ones who had to wait the longest? Scouts, coaches, and spectators never think anything extra special about these players, but they end up being better than the rest of the competition. Nolan Ryan, one of the greatest Major League Baseball pitchers, didn't get drafted until the 12th round. Meaning, 294 other players were chosen before him. Tom Brady, one of the NFL's greatest quarterbacks, had to wait until the 6th round of the draft to be picked #199. What do you think went through their minds as they waited? They may have felt some disappointment, maybe frustration, but I can assure you that their minds were what pushed them to reach heights no one would've ever thought possible after they got their chance. All of their struggles, their patience, and their love for the game would all pay off. They just needed to wait long enough for their opportunity.

Whitney M. Young Jr., an executive director of Civil Rights Organization, The National Urban League, said, "It is better to be prepared for an opportunity and not have one than to have an opportunity and not be prepared." You know, I have heard so many people complain (myself included) that they're "never" going to get the things they want. Maybe you feel it's taking "too long". Too often we forget that the time spent waiting for your first start, your title match, your championship run, etc., might be a blessing. Perhaps you need this time to better prepare for what's ahead. Perhaps you are not ready, and the Universe knows it. Napoleon Hill also says, "... When one is truly ready for a thing, it puts in its appearance."

If the opportunity has not presented itself yet, know that it will. It took three years after I graduated high school for my opportunity to play college football presented itself. I held the thought or idea in my mind, and it materialized. It took a lot longer than expected, but when it showed up, I can truly say I was ready. I had matured mentally, physically, and spiritually. Had I not, I probably would not have learned as much as I did from my experience. At high school graduation I hadn't known about the subconscious mind and how thought is energy vibrating at different frequencies and when our energy matches what we desire, it comes to find us. I had not known that whatever I hold in my mind, will invariably come to me through some odd law which returns that which I think and feel about most. I did not have the knowledge necessary to write this book. I witnessed, with my own eyes, the Law of Attraction at work. Now you are seeing it by reading this book.

Let me suggest to you one last time that there is no such thing as coincidence. It is not coincidence that you are reading this book at the exact moment, in the exact place that you happen to be doing so. Think about how long it's taken you to find this material after all that's happened in your life. Think about your past, what led you to this very moment. The ups and downs, triumphs and setbacks. How many years of civilization, how many generations passed to get to where you are in this exact moment in time? And if you think about your current physical location, how exactly did this book end up in the spot where you are? What brought this book to you? Call it chance, call it guidance, this book, in this very moment, was placed in your hands. Now use it. It is up to **you** to realize your greatest dreams. **Every single one of them**. With faith, visualization, persistence, passion, discipline, affirmations, gratitude and patience, you can and will receive every beautiful thing this life has to offer.

I decided to leave this chapter at the end because I want this to stay fresh in your memory. Everything you have learned means absolutely nothing unless you apply these principles in every area of your life. Greatness doesn't happen overnight. If you truly desire to excel in what you do, it will take time. But as long as you stay internally focused and don't mind the events or people around you, whatever you so dearly long for will be yours.

Try everything you have learned in this book for at least 31 days. Conventional wisdom says it takes about 30 days to form a habit. So what we want to do in these 31 days is make sure we follow every step outlined, while remaining full of confidence and expectancy. I can assure you that as you put in the physical work necessary, your mind and spirit will allow you to improve your game far faster than ever imagined. It's all about keeping that good energy. If, during the next 31 days you follow the principles outlined, you will see just how exceptionally the LoA can and will work in your life.

Now, I am not saying that in the next 31 days you will meet your goal, but I can assure you that in just one month of remaining cognizant of your thoughts and feelings (your energy), you will make huge leaps that bring you closer to what you want.

All of the greats have mastered these principles. They all, whether it seems like it or not visualize, practice and have love for what they do. The funny thing is that most don't even know they're doing it. They have done it for so long that it becomes automatic, a part of them. That may be one reason so many professional athletes become depressed after they retire from sports or competition. That's all they have done for most of their lives!

The patience you possess to get to the level you want will either promote or detract from your success. Patience and practice of physical, mental, and spiritual strength will allow for newly developed habits which will propel you toward your dreams.

Yoda said it best, "**Patience**, you must have, my young padawan." Practice what you've learned and you will receive what your heart desires. Everything. This book was written with sports in mind, but you can apply it to anything else in life. Business, social relationships, family, etc. It all works the same. It all begins in your mind. Your greatness has always been, and will always be, right where you are. Your greatness is within you.

Acknowledgments

Thank you to everyone who supported us throughout the process of writing this book. We wanted to thank Kayla, Mateo, Samuel, Emanuel, Dreax, and every other person who either contributed or aided us on our journey. This one's for you!

About the Authors

Gilbert Villalobos

Born in January 1997, Gilbert's love for Life, sports, and philosophy has always driven him towards self-realization and personal achievement. Having played sports for over 15 years, he loves to watch fellow athletes develop in as many ways possible. He enjoys seeing people grow and his life mission is to bring as many people to God (whoever or whatever that may be) as he can.

If he's not playing flag football on Sunday nights with his best friends, he might be annoying his girlfriend with bad jokes or taking some time to meditate.

His longing for the "Unknown" always sparks new interests and ways of being to live a life full of love and happiness.

Alberto Flores

Alberto Flores was born with a glove in his hand and baseball in his heart. For as long as he can remember, playing baseball was never a dream, but his destiny. Born in Van Nuys, California, his work ethic and love for sports carried him to play Division 1 baseball at California State Northridge where he went on to earn his bachelor's degree in kinesiology.

Now married to Kayla Flores with his three boys

(Mateo, Samuel, and Emanuel), he teaches Physical Education in Arizona and has over 16 years of coaching experience under his belt. Alberto has dedicated his life to make sure athletes of all levels understand that sports is a reflection of the challenges and lessons we learn in everyday life.

Made in the USA
San Bernardino, CA
06 May 2019